"The Notes"

Hey Sis,
With Love^2

Sis

Dr. *Timogi*

#HeySisWithLove^2

#HeySisWithLove²

#HeySisWithLove^2

#HeySisWithLove²

Hey Sis,

You are the gift.

Never forget that.

With love,

Dr. Timogi

#HeySisWithLove^2

Hey Sis,
Some of the worse mind games are the ones we play on ourselves. It's not them (this time) it's you. Free your mind.
With love,
Dr. Timogi

#HeySisWithLove[2]

Hey Sis,
Your perspective of
your story is your
truth, without
debate.
With love,
Dr. Timogi

Hey Sis,
Take your mistake
like a big girl and
redirect your course.
With love,
Dr. Timogi

#HeySisWithLove²

Hey Sis,

It's not failure it's just the end.

With love,

Dr. Timogi

Hey Sis,
He wasn't looking for greener grass, he was looking for cheap turf.
With love,
Dr. Timogi

#HeySisWithLove²

Hey Sis,
Let yourself off with time served. Debt paid. Please, go live your life!
With love,
Dr. Timogi

#HeySisWithLove^2

Hey Sis,

FYI...Narcissist will make you believe their time is priceless and yours ain't worth 2 cents.

With love,

Dr. Timogi

#HeySisWithLove^2

Hey Sis,

His issues were there long before you ever existed and will be there when you leave.

With love,

Dr. Timogi

Hey Sis,

Prayer. Brunch. Therapy. Girl's night. A movie. Shop. Do it ALL in whatever order you choose. Repeat.

With love,
Dr. Timogi

#HeySisWithLove²

Hey Sis,
If people can be
happy without you,
they should.
With love,
Dr. Timogi

#HeySisWithLove²

Hey Sis,

It is not your business
if what's best for you
is not best for them!

With love,

Dr. Timogi

#HeySisWithLove^2

Hey Sis,
Nobody "made you"
the woman you are
except for God
himself.
With love,
Dr. Timogi

#HeySisWithLove^2

Hey Sis,
You're not quitting,
it's already over.
With love,
Dr. Timogi

#HeySisWithLove²

Hey Sis,
Just because the poison hasn't killed you yet doesn't mean you keep drinking it.
With love,
Dr. Timogi

Sis

#HeySisWithLove²

Hey Sis,
Put yourself first today so you can be here alive AND well tomorrow.
With love,
Dr. Timogi

#HeySisWithLove²

Hey Sis,

Pandemic: Making your entire world revolve around someone else's illness.

With love,
Dr. Timogi

#HeySisWithLove^2

Hey Sis,

They were there for your pain but not for your promotion because your pain made them feel powerful and your promotion makes them ~~jealous~~ show their true colors.

With love,
Dr. Timogi

#HeySisWithLove²

Hey Sis,

If you were worthless,
they wouldn't have
spent so much time
trying to make you
think you were.

With love,

Dr. Timogi

#HeySisWithLove²

Hey Sis,
Love the hate that
made you great!
With love,
Dr. Timogi

#HeySisWithLove²

Hey Sis,
The first step to getting it together is taking the first step.
With love,
Dr. Timogi

#HeySisWithLove²

Hey Sis,
What "was" has
drastically changed.
Now you must too.
With love,
Dr. Timogi

#HeySisWithLove²

Hey Sis,
It's mentally,
spiritually, and
emotionally
detrimental to give
more than you have.
With love,
Dr. Timogi

#HeySisWithLove²

Hey Sis,
You never need
permission to turn to
the next page,
chapter, or book of
your life.
With love,
Dr. Timogi

#HeySisWithLove^2

Hey Sis,
You are responsible
for creating your
peace one decision at
a time.
With love,
Dr. Timogi

#HeySisWithLove^2

Hey Sis,
How many more
times can you justify
this mess? Your move.
With love,
Dr. Timogi

Sis

#HeySisWithLove^2

Hey Sis,

So, what if he did change for her? He made it perfectly clear he wasn't gonna change for you.

With love,

Dr. Timogi

Hey Sis,

He.

Didn't.

Want.

You.

With love,

Dr. Timogi

#HeySisWithLove^2

Hey Sis,
Sparing the pain of a grown man by inflicting pain on yourself is unhealthy.
With love,
Dr. Timogi

#HeySisWithLove^2

Hey Sis,

That's your phone.

You pay the bill. You

choose when to

answer it and when

not to.

With love,

Dr. Timogi

#HeySisWithLove²

Hey Sis,
I support you in your decision to work toward your holistic health.
With love,
Dr. Timogi

#HeySisWithLove²

Hey Sis,

They told you. They showed you. They wrote it in a text. Made a meme. Made a gif. And, left a voicemail. (An actual voicemail!) Your move.

With love,

Dr. Timogi

#HeySisWithLove^2

Hey Sis,

Life is too short to convince anyone of anything. Go live!

With love,

Dr. Timogi

#HeySisWithLove^2

Hey Sis,

If losing them brings you peace then what did you really lose? Lemme help; nothing sis, you lost nothing, ab-so-lute-ly nothing!

With love,

Dr. Timogi

#HeySisWithLove²

Hey Sis,
You do not have to
have a perfect past to
deserve a beautiful
future.
With love,
Dr. Timogi

#HeySisWithLove²

Hey Sis,
Their behavior is not rejection it's acknowledgement; they don't deserve you.
With love,
Dr. Timogi

#HeySisWithLove²

Hey Sis,
Folks aren't judging your choice – they're envying your freedom.
With love,
Dr. Timogi

#HeySisWithLove^2

Hey Sis,

Yes, it's hard to walk away. You know what's harder, staying; staying sad, staying broke, busted, and disgusted, forever. That's hard.

With love,

Dr. Timogi

#HeySisWithLove²

Hey Sis,
You don't need
anyone's permission
to create happiness in
your life.
With love,
Dr. Timogi

#HeySisWithLove^2

Hey Sis,

It's a lie that no one else will want you but for the record; "No One" is an upgrade in this case.

With love,

Dr. Timogi

#HeySisWithLove²

Hey Sis,
He is what he ain't
and that's all he's
going to be.
With love,
Dr. Timogi

#HeySisWithLove²

Hey Sis,

It can be better. A whole lot better. And it will be when you decide you're ready to make it better by whatever actions BETTER requires of YOU.

With love,

Dr. Timogi

#HeySisWithLove²

Hey Sis,
Now you know you should open those blinds and eat something. Call me. I got you. No questions asked.
With love,
Dr. Timogi

#HeySisWithLove²

Hey Sis,

This situation is not a rejection it's God's protection.

With love,

Dr. Timogi

Sis

#HeySisWithLove²

Hey Sis,
Choose alone over desperate every time.
With love,
Dr. Timogi

#HeySisWithLove²

Hey Sis,

His representative has left the relationship. You now have who you're gonna have. This IS his true self. So, honor your true self.

With love,
Dr. Timogi
#HeySisWithLove²

Hey Sis,
Self-care is not a
luxury or an option
it's a vital necessity.
With love,
Dr. Timogi

#HeySisWithLove[2]

Hey Sis,
I support you in
making decisions that
put your mental
health first.
With love,
Dr. Timogi

#HeySisWithLove²

Hey Sis,
I support you in your
choice to heal.
With love,
Dr. Timogi

#HeySisWithLove²

Hey Sis,
No explanation
required. We get it.
We were waiting for
you to get it.
With love,
Dr. Timogi

#HeySisWithLove²

Hey Sis,
The best thing
another person can
do for you is to show
you clearly, they do
not choose you.
With love,
Dr. Timogi

Sis

#HeySisWithLove²

Hey Sis,
Today, choose your truth, your peace, and your joy over pacifying a whole grown-up.
With love,
Dr. Timogi

#HeySisWithLove²

Hey Sis,
It takes the **right two**
to make a thing go
right. You're only one.
With love,
Dr. Timogi

#HeySisWithLove²

Hey Sis,

It's your car, your lane, and your gas. Drive as fast or slow as you want but drive toward your desired goal.

With love,
Dr. Timogi

#HeySisWithLove²

Hey Sis,
Wanting you silent is the same as wanting you dead.
With love,
Dr. Timogi

#HeySisWithLove^2

Hey Sis,
Mama had to live
with her choices, but
you don't. Make your
own.
With love,
Dr. Timogi

#HeySisWithLove²

Hey Sis,

The same motive you used to walk in is the same motive you use to walk out; "What do I need now?"

With love,

Dr. Timogi

#HeySisWithLove²

Hey Sis,

If they're headed nowhere tell me again why you're still there?

With love,

Dr. Timogi

#HeySisWithLove²

Hey Sis,
Please admit you
made a mistake so
you can make your
next move.
With love,
Dr. Timogi

#HeySisWithLove²

Hey Sis,

Hate does not edify.

Healing does.

With love,

Dr. Timogi

#HeySisWithLove²

Hey Sis,
Be wary of those
present for your
misery and not for
your victory.
With love,
Dr. Timogi

#HeySisWithLove²

Hey Sis,

Lonely is good. In that space you learn the ability to love yourself as unconditionally as you have loved others.

With love,

Dr. Timogi

#HeySisWithLove²

Hey Sis,
Growth is for grown-
ups. Be one cause
they sure ain't.
With love,
Dr. Timogi

#HeySisWithLove²

Hey Sis,
You're doing worse
with them than you
were without them.
You're welcome.
With love,
Dr. Timogi

Sis

#HeySisWithLove²

Hey Sis,

Narcissist: A person who will give nothing while expecting everything and that still ain't enough.

With love,

Dr. Timogi

#HeySisWithLove²

Hey Sis,
Healing is uncomfortable at first and the gratification won't be instant, but it will be worth it.
With love,
Dr. Timogi

#HeySisWithLove²

Hey Sis,
You know good and
well this ain't going
to work. Call me
when you accept it.
(Lunch on me.)
With love,
Dr. Timogi

#HeySisWithLove²

Hey Sis,
The first person you owe anything to is yourself. You owe her peace, you owe her joy, and you owe her your best life.
With love,
Dr. Timogi

#HeySisWithLove²

Hey Sis,
If you settle you
suffocate. If you wait
you win. I promise.
With love,
Dr. Timogi

#HeySisWithLove²

Hey Sis,

I know you're not ok right now. That's ok. I also know you're going to be. I'm here for you.

With love,

Dr. Timogi

#HeySisWithLove²

Hey Sis,
Mama used her
strength to endure so
you could use yours
to leave; not repeat.
With love,
Dr. Timogi

#HeySisWithLove^2

Hey Sis,

Pandemic: Thinking all men in the world are the same when they're not so you stay with your current virus.

With love,

Dr. Timogi

#HeySisWithLove²

Hey Sis,
Set your self-love
boundary and don't
move the line to
accommodate
anyone!
With love,
Dr. Timogi

#HeySisWithLove²

Hey Sis,

The best thing to do after a making a bad choice is to make a good choice.

With love,

Dr. Timogi

#HeySisWithLove^2

Hey Sis,
If you have to explain
yourself to people,
they're not your
people.
With love,
Dr. Timogi

#HeySisWithLove²

Hey Sis,

Be patient. You're not broken; you're evolving.

With love,

Dr. Timogi

Hey Sis,
They don't hate you.
They hate their lack
of what maintains,
sustains, and
empowers you.
With love,
Dr. Timogi

#HeySisWithLove²

Hey Sis,
You survived a
pandemic. Surely you
can survive a damn
ignant.
With love,
Dr. Timogi

Sis

#HeySisWithLove^2

Hey Sis,

Wear that dress!

Having life today is a special occasion.

Where we going?

With love,

Dr. Timogi

#HeySisWithLove²

Hey Sis,

Narcissist: They have feelings, you don't. But if you do, your feelings don't matter. (Because they caused them.) Only theirs are important. So, pacify them, now! Through your own pain. Without complaint.

With love,

Dr. Timogi

#HeySisWithLove^2

Hey Sis,

Stop.

Making.

Excuses.

For.

Them.

With love,

Dr. Timogi

#HeySisWithLove^2

Hey Sis,

Say it: My mental health comes first. Repeat it until you get it. Now, seek the help you need.

With love,

Dr. Timogi

#HeySisWithLove²

Hey Sis,
Your healing is in
front of you not
behind you.
With love,
Dr. Timogi

#HeySisWithLove^2

Hey Sis,

Do not sentence yourself to a life of guaranteed misery out of fear or embarrassment.

With love,

Dr. Timogi

#HeySisWithLove^2

Hey Sis,

Ask yourself...Would you still choose them today?

With love,

Dr. Timogi

Hey Sis,
The first person you have to take care of should always be you.
With love,
Dr. Timogi

Sis

#HeySisWithLove^2

Hey Sis,
Therapy is not for the weak, it's for grown-ups. Get you some!
With love,
Dr. Timogi

#HeySisWithLove²

Hey Sis,

Time does not heal.

The truth,

accountability and

responsibility over

time heals.

With love,

Dr. Timogi

#HeySisWithLove²

Hey Sis,
He could have had it
all. You still can. Go
get your blessing.
With love,
Dr. Timogi

#HeySisWithLove²

Hey Sis,

Be patient with yourself, you're becoming the woman you need to be to create your joy!

With love,

Dr. Timogi

#HeySisWithLove²

Hey Sis,
Today is the day. Not
tomorrow, not next
week, not next year,
today. Don't postpone
your breakthrough!
With love,
Dr. Timogi

#HeySisWithLove²

Hey Sis,

A-lone is better than;

A-liar, A-loser, A-cheater, A-jerk, A-waste of time.

(Seriously)! A-men.

With love,

Dr. Timogi

#HeySisWithLove²

Hey Sis,
They been wearing a mask and social distancing way before the pandemic.
With love,
Dr. Timogi

#HeySisWithLove²

Hey Sis,

Leaving behind what
doesn't serve you does not
(1) require an
announcement
(2) have to be cosigned, or
(3) be glamorous.
It just has to be done.
With love,
Dr. Timogi

Sis

#HeySisWithLove^2

Hey Sis,

A lesson learned late is better than a lesson ignored or not learned at all. Take heed.

With love,

Dr. Timogi

#HeySisWithLove^2

Hey Sis,

Don't let your intellect betray you by over analyzing the obvious. It is exactly what you know it is.

With love,

Dr. Timogi

#HeySisWithLove²

Hey Sis,

Only the currencies of mental and physical health will allow you to enjoy monetary wealth.

With love,

Dr. Timogi

#HeySisWithLove^2

Hey Sis,

Your lack of perfection doesn't justify their lack of commitment and abuse.

With love,

Dr. Timogi

#HeySisWithLove²

Hey Sis,

The Lord giveth and
the Lord taketh away
so just wave!
With love,
Dr. Timogi

#HeySisWithLove^2

Hey Sis,
When they play the God card remind them, He doesn't gamble.
With love,
Dr. Timogi

#HeySisWithLove²

"The Notes"

Hey Sis, With Love²

Dr. *Timogi*

#HeySisWithLove²

Hey Sis,

Thank you for joining the #heysiswithlove movement. This book is for any woman who ever thought it was only her going through it. We are healing. Together. Post your favorite note with the hashtag #HeySisWithLove. Visit my website. Dr. Timogi.com to email me via the contact form. I hope this book is a gift to every woman who reads it.

With love,

Dr. Timogi

#HeySisWithLove²

Hey Sis,

Write your own notes!

With love,

Dr. Timogi

Sis

#HeySisWithLove²

#HeySisWithLove²

www.ingramcontent.com/pod-product-compliance
Lightning Source LLC
Chambersburg PA
CBHW072206270326
41930CB00011B/2549